I0765709
THIS BOOK
BELONGS TO..

Color This Page

Color This Page

Color This Page

Color This Page

Color This Page

Color This Page

Color This Page

Color This Page

Color This Page

Color This Page

Color This Page

Color This Page

Color This Page

Color This Page

Color This Page

CoLor This Page

Color This Page

Color This Page

Color This Page

CoLor This Page

Color This Page

Color This Page

Color This Page

Color This Page

Color This Page

Color This Page

Color This Page

CoLor This Page

Color This Page

Color This Page

Color This Page

CoLor This Page

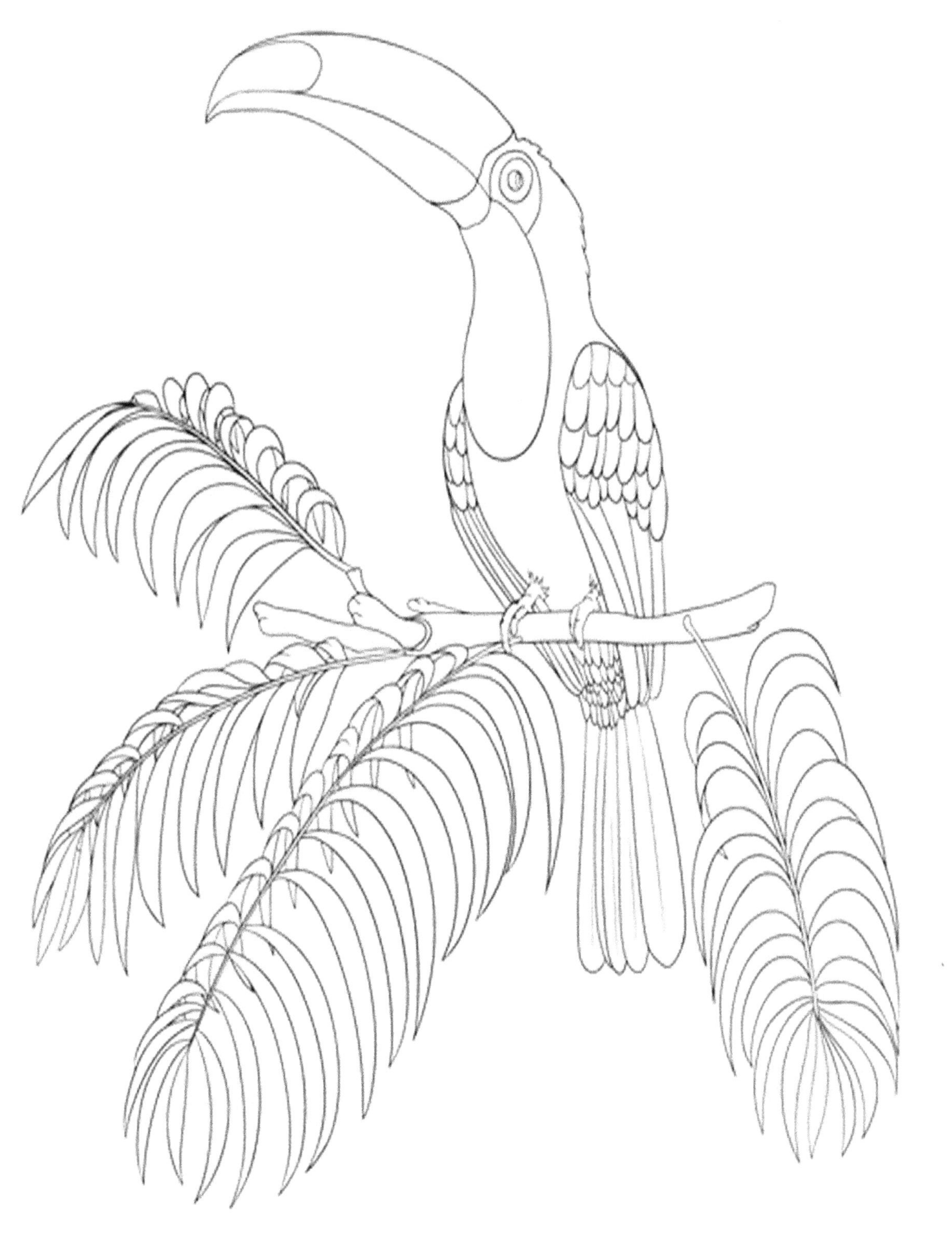

Color This Page

Color This Page

COLOR THIS PAGE